Tavern Talk

Old Taverns and Tales in Springfield Illinois

By Bobby & Sandy Orr
Springfield Illinois

outskirts
press

DEDICATION

We dedicate this book to Sandy's Dad, Mr. Bob Vose the "Korn-Dog King". Bob delivered Ice for the American Ice Company located at 1001 E Miller, later the Union Ice company at 918 Edwards for several years before going to work for the City of Springfield as a meter reader. He boasts of being in the basement of every Tavern in town, although he was a non-drinker. While Bob is best known for his Illinois State Fair Corn-Dogs and being a City Alderman representing Ward 5, Bob's love for the City of Springfield led him to a lifetime of dedication to the preservation of the rich history our City. He inspired us and was an enormous help recalling the names and addresses of many of the businesses listed in "Tavern Talk."

Thank you Dad.
Love
Sandy & Bobby

On The Cover: The Curve Inn, 3219 S 6ᵗʰ St. circa 1940's
Inside Cover: Mary Manci and her son Louie Jr. in front of the HI D Ho Tavern 1800 E Adams 1948

Just a disclaimer footnote; this book was compiled from several sources many of whom had been drinking so it's possible we didn't get something 100% accurate. We recognize not every tavern is listed here and some are not technically within the Springfield City limits; we are planning a second book, Tavern Talk II that will include establishments all over Sangamon County IL. as well as any additions and corrections brought to our attention. Follow us on Facebook at "Springfield Tavern History " or e-mail us at Taverntalkspi@gmail.com

Enjoy the History

PHOTOGRAPH CREDIT

Sangamon Valley Collection, Lincoln Library Springfield, Illinois

Louie Manci Jr.

Claudio Pecori

Haroldene Antonaci

Tom Blasko

Illinois State Journal-Register

Table of Contents

Tavern Talk

Springfield Illinois truly has a rich history of locally owned Taverns.

Partners, conglomerates, shareholders and corporations own many of the bars and restaurants we enjoy today. But, back in the day, it wasn't unusual even common for a family to live in the back of or above their family owned tavern. I can vividly remember **Mike and Dea's Tavern** (Mike Ushman and Dea Galassi) **at 2790 Fox road; that's before Walt and Dene Antonacci** took it over in 1963. Dea would shuffle out of her attached house through a doorway with just a curtain draped over the opening to serve the neighborhood folks a cold beer or a sandwich. Everyone did know everyone else; it was a neighborhood tavern and everyone in the neighborhood was welcome, kids too.

The tavern business was an honorable one; husband and wife worked it together and everyone respected that. The proprietor wore a crisply pressed white shirt with a bleached white apron. It seems to me at least in Springfield; taverns were set up like a local church parish. People worked, worshiped and socialized together, their kids went to church and school together.

If you lived south, Laketown, Southern View or in the Cabbage Patch your dad or maybe your mom may have worked at Allis Chalmers and you shopped at Castors Grocery store on Linn Street.

You would have been a customer of Whalen Drug store, Watt Brothers Pharmacy, or Homeier's dairy at 900 Stanford; you and or your children went to Southern View, Staley, Harvard Park, Little Flower, Jefferson or Feitshans, and your dad (and mom) drank a cold draught beer after work and cashed his paycheck on a Friday night at one of the nearby taverns outside the A-C gate.

Depending on which department you worked at Allis Chalmers that's the gate you entered and left after your shift, your lunch bucket subject to inspection by security. **Johnny and VI's Tavern** located at 2800 So. 11th (later **One-Eye-Jacks**) was located near the 11th Street gates, **Enders Tavern,** 1047 Stanford and **Charlie Zaubie's** 1041 Stanford were located conveniently near the Stanford St gates. Jack Hagen owned the **Lake Springfield Tavern** 1221 Linn St and the **Curve Inn** owned in the earlier years by Guido and Celeste Manci located at 3219 So. 6th St Road took care of the A-C, Bunn Corporation, F S (Farm Supply) and Pegwell Pete's workers to the south. Many of these large manufacturers worked three shifts, so the taverns were open 24/7 to accommodate their friends. Nearby taverns actively supported the UAW local #1027 union workers when they were on strike for months at a time, extending credit to their friends and customers.

Millie's Sunset Inn a tavern located at 3540 So 6th St Road catered to the construction workers and others; Its still there with a different owner. If you were under age, Millie (Mildred Ostenburg) might serve you a warm Stag beer if you sat there and kept your mouth shut.

What a different time in life. People didn't need much; they worked hard, earned their money and spent it in their neighborhood. Some people condemned the "tavern life" and I assume in some cases with just cause however I believe the vast majority of local tavern customers are some of the nicest, hard working real folks your will ever meet.

It was the same scenario for workers at Sangamo Electric, Pillsbury Mill, Weavers manufacturing and others in and around the great City of Springfield. Just think of how much product was produced in the Springfield area alone. Springfield was also home of Franklin Life Insurance Company, a world leader in the insurance industry.

Times have changed and the rules have changed too! Does anyone recall getting a ride home from the police when you had one too many?

Don't get us wrong, impaired driving is a very serious matter and should not be tolerated. However these days it is an economic engine for law enforcement agencies, income from DUI fines providing funds for a large part of their budgets. I remember the Lake Police would confiscate your beer if you were underage and sent you on your way. I wonder where all that confiscated beer from the lake park areas went? (Ever hear of the W-L club? (Water & Light)

Part of the beauty of neighborhood taverns was that people didn't have to drive, they walked or rode with their neighbor; folks didn't have multiple cars. As a kid I lived in the Cabbage Patch, I remember riding my bike to **Lakeside Package Liquor** at 2315 E Linn St. (Stevenson Drive) with a note from my Mom to get a ½ jug of Pabst and a pack of Pall Mall cigarettes. I got a stern warning too; don't break the Jug!

Walt and Dene Antonacci 2790 Fox Road (1963)

Buster Connors
Tavern 1100 E Ash St.

Old Time Taverns-Then and Now

Enders Tavern at 1047 Stanford has the oldest liquor license in the city. Current owner Tom Enders tells us his Grandfather who was the first owner ordered the first two kegs of beer delivered in the city after prohibition. Can you think of any other Taverns still at the same location with the same name for 70 + years? How about these;

- **Enders Tavern**-1047 Stanford (Still owned by the same family)
- **Cottage Inn** 922 No. MacArthur (although it was located at another address briefly)
- **Illinois Tap** 715 No. Grand Ave East
- **Lake Springfield Tavern** 1215 (Linn St.) Stevenson Dr.
- **Brooklyn Tavern** 1901 S. 15th, St.
- **Curve Inn** 3219 S 6th St.

I guess we can add the **Old Lux** at 1900 So 15th St too. Ownership has obviously changed for some over the years but the taverns still stand where they have for many years; that's History!

Some places come and go, some went with the help of the city's "urban development".

Do You Remember "**The Levee**"? Some of you will if you were born before 1950, some of you might not admit it! The "Levee" stretched from about 10th Street to the East, 3rd Street to the West mostly on 5th, Washington, Jefferson and Adams Streets.

Do you remember a few of those historic places?

- **The Alton Lounge** 315 E Washington
- **The Argone** 407 E Jefferson
- **Bakers Tap** 100 E Jefferson
- **Bimbo Club** 723 E Washington
- **The Derby** 411 E Jefferson
- **The Diamond Club** 721 E Washington
- **Floyd's Tap Room** 405 E Jefferson
- **Gee I Tavern then D-T's** at 212 N 5th
- **Junior's Tavern** 205 E Washington
- **Lapinski's** 1030 E Washington
- **The Last Word** 411 E Washington
- **Mel's Club** 729 E Washington
- **Paddock** 322 E Jefferson
- **Palm Room** 817 E Washington

- **The Town Pump** 306 E Washington
- **The Winsor** 432 E Monroe
- **Wonder Inn** 808 E Washington
- **Club Lido** 416 E Capital Ave.
- The **Circus-Circus** was located at 115 N 7th
- **The Saddle Club** 307 S 6th and **The Press Box** at 520 E Monroe on the alley
- The **Pre View Lounge (Later the Lori-al)** at 427 E Jefferson

The bar inside the **Lori-Al** had an extended and rounded center section of the bar for the dancers. A gentleman named Dick Austin's mother owned the Lori-Al; he held a high level position in the Federal government back in the day. That actual bar is now located in the **Alamo** at 115 N 5th. Just think of the elbows that rested on the rail and dollar bills that have passed over that bar.

We were told some of the Levee taverns on the north side of Washington Street were owned or frequented mostly by black families and the taverns on the south side were owned or frequented by white mostly immigrant families. An author named Martha Miller wrote a book in 2005 about the levee from 1965-1976, she described it as "Springfield's seedy section". Louie Manci Jr. the current owner of **"Louie's Bar and Beer Garden" 3110 Stanton Street** recalls selling "The Register" newspaper while in grade school on the levee and was welcome on both sides of the street. Louie said, "We were not black or white, they were all in the same business and everyone respected everyone else, I was always treated very well". **Cansler's Lounge,** owned by an African American gentleman Mr. Les Cansler was between 8th and 9th on Washington back in the day. Some racist threw a Molotov cocktail into what they thought was Cansler's, but they hit the wrong tavern; serves them right! Cansler's Cafe was also located at 307 E Washington. Some people think the levee ghosts still haunt 5th street downtown Springfield. There were a lot more so called "levee" taverns. Some older taverns you may associate with the Levee could be considered downtown taverns; they survived demolition when the Levee and Orpheum Theater were demolished and Horace Mann was built as well as other downtown Springfield expansions.

Argonne Tavern 407 E Jefferson-

Argonne Tavern –John Mezo Owner (1933)

Preview Lounge (later the Lori-Al) 427 E Jefferson

The Last Word 411 E Washington

Downtown Area Taverns

These include; **Machino's** at 400 E Adams, now **J.P. Kelly's, The Towne Lounge** at 214 N 4th. Buster DiNora owned the Towne Lounge and rumors say he was considered the godfather of the Levee. The **So-Ho** at 139 N 4th, **Charlottes 113 Club** (later **Kane's and the Alamo**) at 113-115 N 5th, **Smokey's Den** at 127 N 5th. **The Orpheum Lounge** at 208 N 5th and the **Whirlaway** 214 N 5th; the **Century Lounge** was located at 217 N 5th.

Other great downtown taverns were close; **The Old Hogan Brothers (Skube's)** at 106 N 6th. **The Eagle Grill and Tavern, Luke's Monarch,** and the **Lincoln Square Tavern** at 112 N 6th St. Don't forget **Farhrenbockers, The Palace, Crystal Tavern, Opal's and Murphy's** all located on North 6th St. T**he Piccadilly** liquor store was also located at 109 N 5th Street. **The Jackson Club** was located at 505 E Madison for many years. We found the **Wooden Shoe** later called the **Tami Ami** and **the Dome** at 121 N 5th St. **Frank Marconi's** later **Duffy's** was located at 118 N 7th, and **Marconi's Gay 90's club** was located at 120 N 7th, next to the **Hitching Post** at 128 N 7th

People should remember one location that produced several fun taverns; 117 North 2nd Street was **Luttrell's Red Tavern** and was later **Miss Kitty's** owned by Kitty Heckenkamp. After that it was the **2nd Street Pub,** when Miss Kitty's moved a block away to 131 E Jefferson which at one time was **Impastato's Lounge;** she called it **Kitty's Courthouse**. Located at 126 E Jefferson was **Greta's** then the **Romanesque** then **Viele's Planet.**

A name to remember in the Springfield tavern business was Vito Impastato. He began tavern ownership in the 1930's with **Club Holiday** on N MacArthur and No. Grand, he later operated **The Orchid Lounge** for over 20 years, and **The Supper Club**. (See these places mentioned in other sections as well) Mr. Impastato was suspected of an association with organized crime however he was never convicted of a serious crime.

Some of the downtown hotels had taverns located inside that were both elegant and available to the local's not just travelers. **The Hotel Governor** was home to the **Organ Grinder, The Leland Hotel** had the **Red Lion** and a Springfield Classic the **St. Nicholas Hotel** had **The Glade. The Elks Club** was located at 509 South 6th until 1979 and had several interior member only bars like **The Walnut Room, & The Cottonwood room.**

Springfield Elks Lodge #158 now located at 409 East Lake Shore Dr. was the former home of the **Springfield Lake Shore Club Inc.** until 1979.

Monarch Tavern
110 N Sixth

The Grand Inn Ash & MacArthur- Eddie Eck owner (1939)

Canselers Lounge 807 E Washington Les Cansler Owner

The LeLand Hotel between 5ᵗʰ and 6ᵗʰ on Capitol (1916)

The Proud North End Taverns

If you are or were a "North Ender" you're a proud member of the great history of our community. As we said in the introduction, not unlike the south end, industry was thriving in the North End of Springfield; Pillsbury Mill and Sangamo Electric helped to support these hard working families, and the local tavern owner worked to support the quality of life these hard workers needed to carry on. Some of these local taverns were;

- **Dorsey's, Maple Gardens** and later the **Jolly Cork** were located at 1157 N 1st St.
- **Val Schmitt** operated a tavern at 215 N 2nd St., still in operation; this was later **Delaney's Cabin** and for many years was **Sweed's Butternut Hut**, later bought by Bob and Betty Stoepler, **Bob's Butternut Hut.**
- **Shokers** was located at 542 N 2nd Street, and the **Gin Mill** was located at 648 N 2nd later **Beckner's tavern**.
- **The Hide out** later **the Firehouse** was located at 2237 North 3rd St, The Firehouse burned down! Go figure!
- **Delaney's** owned by a few folks over the years is still located at 2249 N 3rd Street.
- On North 4th Street you would find **Pappy's,** later **Jim's Lounge; Tom and Charlie's** was located at 119 N 4th.
- **Opal's, Bob's and Jeayne's** was located at 209 N 6th
- **The Loft** was located at 2207 N 5th, and **the Fairview Club** at 2437 N 5th.

Franny's deserves a special commendation, did you know before it was Franny's at 2136 N 8th Street it was **the Fairground Beer Garden, Twin Pine Inn and Jink's.** Someone said it was also called the Bus Stop.

Stevie's Latin Village was located at 620 N 9th **Riccardo's later Ragazzi's** was located at 1614 N 9th

Nearby North 11th Street was home to several great taverns; at 704 N 11th, there was the **Rose Bud, Ed and Nannies, Cody's Inn and the Little Indian.**

At 1630 N 11th, **the North Pole**, I believe owned by the Marconi family, after that **The Spa, Lazar's, and The Canopy.**

Casper's, E & J and Dudes were at 2001 N 11th; I'm not sure if the **Red Onion** was there or at 2143 N 11th where it was **Bucari's, The Main Gate, Russell's, the Blue Bayou and Jimmez & company.**

Don't forget, **Alby's Tavern** located at 600 N 14th or 1400 E Carpenter. **Wally's tavern** was located at 716 N 14th and a block over at 906 N 15th Street was **The Mill.** The tavern at 2323 N 15th was **Butch and Ester's, Art and Betty's, Butch's Place and Cheers.**

When my good friend Butch Staber sold his bar to Cheers, he opened his place **Butchs 19th Hole** at 1247 North 19th Street and has been there for over 30 years. Prior to his ownership the place was **George and Jonnies and Parkers Lounge**. This was across the tracks from **Viola's** at 1222 North 19th St.

Franny's Tavern 8th and Sangamon

On the N/E corner of 19th and North Grand I'm told **Mary's Friendly Tavern**. Mary and her husband Nick operated the tavern it's a gas Station now. The story goes if you caused trouble in Mary's Friendly Tavern you were literally thrown out the front door and the place was so close to North Grand Ave. you landed in the street.

What would North End Tavern's be without those located on North Grand Avenue; Places like**; The Maple Gardens** at 116, **The Oasis** at 120, **Maisenbacher's** at 610 and **the Cara-Sel** at 625 E North Grand Ave. As we said in the introduction the **Illinois Tap** is still in its original location at 715 No Grand Ave East, Sandy's Uncle Jim Vose was an owner at one time. **Lawson's** was located at 726, and at 1024 No Grand Ave East it was **Phil and Mary's, Midges Place, and the North Grand Pub.**

Marcy's and the Trio Lounge was at 1030 North Grand Ave next door to **Slim and Jerry's.**

Going the other way toward Grandview Jimmy Richards operated **Kie's** at 2031 North Grand Ave East where he served a great bowl of Chili and a brunswager sandwich. The glass block bar leaned so far to the east in later years you had to eat your chili from east to west. With a wonderful lunch at Kie's there was no need for probiotics (if you know what I mean). Jimmy's daughter Becky Richards Donely wrote to us and shared that her grandfather and uncle Russ Richards owned the tavern before Jimmy, Russ lived in a house near the tavern, where the flower shop is now. Russ Richards also had a tavern in Grandview where the B G Café was before it burned down, and don't forget Grandview was "dry" for a period of time.

Just off North Grand at 1135 N 6th Street by the RR tracks was the **County Cork Pub.** Although not a real old time tavern, it was well known and usually packed with AAA Cardinals baseball players and Nurses on shift work at the nearby hospitals hoping to marry a major league baseball player. Great Place! Before it was the County Cork it was **Moore's Tavern and Beechlers.**

A popular place called **Biggie's and Bubba's** popped up for a short while at ^{1st} and Carpenter Street, Al Ecoff managed it, not sure who actually owned it.

Not unlike a lot of kids born in the 50's you too were part of the neighborhood tavern. Larry Ray a proud North ender wrote to us detailing his stories about his times at the **Millview Tavern** at 1522 Moffat now **Mafat's**. The current owner of 18 years still lives next door just like the old days. Don't confuse the Millview with **the Mill**, both within clear view of Pillsbury mill. The **Silver Moon** was located at 1537 E Moffat.

The Lazy Lu was and still is just up the street at 19th and Moffat across the RR tracks. The original owners had one of the first liquor licenses in town, the place has since been sold.

Can anyone discuss the tavern business without mentioning the name **Bob Schleyhann!** The guy is a legend and I had the honor and privilege of knowing him and his family. In fact he's the one who was dragging me into all those social clubs. What a man; he owned **The Ranch House** at 1236 North Walnut before in burned down. We are unable to tell all the Ranch House Stories, I'll bet some of them are true.

The Cave, was a tavern just across the street from the Ranch House on N Walnut..

Other taverns on North Walnut were; **Cactus Charlie's** at 1701 N Walnut and at 3600 N Walnut you would have found **Stork Club, Bob's Chuck Wagon, Frank and Marge's, Kenny and Velma's, Phelmans and the Runway Tavern.**

Lawsons Tavern 726 N Grand Ave E

Maple Gardens Monument Ave and N Grand

While not really identified as North End Taverns in Devereaux Heights-Peoria Road and 31ˢᵗ Street (Dirksen Parkway) you would have found several great places;

- **The Jail House** owned by Eva Antonnacci
- **The Mecca**, **Welch's, Gordon and Betty's and Walt's Inn** were at 1701 Peoria road.
- **Horins Inn** at 1905 Peoria Rd
- Gary Sullivan wrote to us and told us about **Sully's, Sullivan's Shanty, later the Row-D-Dow** was at 1937 Peoria Road, now Jungle Jims.
- **Big John's, Wanda's Zoo and Quality liquors** were at the site of **Knuckleheads** at 2000 Peoria Rd; **Vic and Mary's later Vic's Pizza** a Springfield pizza icon was located at 2025 Peoria Rd.
- Another Icon, **the Skyrocket** was located at 2202 Peoria road.
- At 2300 Peoria Rd **The Blue Moon, later Wanda's corner and the Stadium** still stands.

It appears several taverns were located at 2724 Peoria Road, **Happy Landing, Midiri's, Buzzys, Dug out, Bonnie's and the City's edge**. The **City's Edge** was built and owned by Kenny Vose, Tom Allard.

At 2801 Peoria Rd were **Fidlers, Jack and Dottie's, Sully's** (or was this Sullivan's Shanty) **and Parkers**.

Located at 3036 Peoria Rd. was **The Wishing Well** owned by Marino Mazzini, **Billy's II, Bobby's A Dance Bar and Zoo Babies** and at 4000 Peoria Rd was **Dodd's 4000 Club**. The **Mighty Fine** owned by Tony and Josephine Lovecho was located at 3045

Sangamon Ave. The **Koo Koo's Nest** owned by Gary Best is now the **Stockyards Saloon,** it opened there in 2018 after a rumored squabble between Gary Best and building owner Wanda Sacccaro.

The **Roll Inn** was located at 3703 N Dirksen and don't forget a fun place the **Longbranch,** located at 2221 N Dirksen. The **Horseshoe Lounge later Bev's Corral** was located at 1914 N Dirksen; the **My Way Lounge** at 2909 N Dirksen.

Donangelo's was at 404 N Dirksen.

Although not an old time tavern Mic and Karey Wanless started a new trend opening **Northern Lights** at 500 N Dirksen Parkway in a strip mall. That trend caught on in Springfield. Mic now owns **Westwoods Lodge** on West Jefferson, formally the **Fox Run.**

Do you remember the **Bundox Hickory Pit or the No Place Pub** at 301 N Dirksen?

Special mention on Peoria Road, **Chuck Weyants Holiday Inn at** 4230 and at 4230 1/2 Peoria Rd was **Stooges.** Billy Barr owned a place called **The Tumbleweed** located on Mayden Ave.

Way up the bend almost to the four corners, at 3700 N Dirksen was **Missionary Mary's,** and a place called **The Bimini Club** was located on N 8ᵗʰ Street Rd., the Cellini brothers owned it.

The Sky Rocket 2202 Peoria Road

Taverns Were Scattered in the Neighborhoods

Moving south of downtown and in any direction you were likely to find a local neighborhood tavern. You have to remember the " West side" so to speak ended near Chatham road; in fact that was almost the country. Rt. 4, Chatham Road was a major north south highway before I-55 was constructed. **Grier's Village Inn** at 1305 Wabash was pretty far west, and a tavern nicknamed the **Chicken Coop** (no address, except "Decatur Road") located on east cook near where Cook and Rt. 36 met was pretty far east. A story told of the "Chicken Coop" was that range chickens and goats ran loose outside this tavern. Back in the day license plates were made from a soy bean-based material during the war and the goats ate the license plates from the cars parked at the tavern. (Hey who knows!)

There were and still are some great local tavern owners on the east side of Springfield. Cozy Coe operated a few taverns and social clubs, Chuck Hunter was a name to know and of-course Macarthur "Mac" Frazier, owned and operated **Macs Lounge** at 1231 E Cook, before it was Macs it was also **Rawls Lounge and Saner's.** Also on Cook Street was **Webb's Corner and the Metropolitan Liquor and Lounge at** 1418 E Cook, **Gentile's Tavern** at 1420 E Cook and at 1801 E Cook was the **Palm Café, Russo's and Booda's Lounge.** The **Hi "D" Ho,** as shown on the inside cover originally owned by the Manci family was at 18th and Adams, but **The Hi De Ho** was later re-located at 1801 E Cook**.**

The Rose Bowl Club was at 2501 E Cook, now a church, and the **Green Winnie** formally the **Redwood Lounge** was located at 2805 E Cook.

The Track Shack is still at 233 E Laurel it was **Reno's Tavern** before the track shack. Mimi Vitalie owned the track shack in those days. And don't forget just down the road on Laurel at the 10 ½ street track's was **Ernie and Yvonne's, Shirley's, Duffy's Bernie and Jake's and Gloria's,** all located at 1009 E Laurel.

Near West Cook at 701 S 9th was **Bob's Corner** later **Dino's Lounge.** Rumor has it that a local resident operated and distributed several coin operated vending machines from Bob's Corner; some say he was cutting into another gaming company's territory and ultimately he was murdered for it. A dog found his head and authorities were alerted.

1800 E Brown is the location for several taverns; Back in "38" **William Stallone** operated a tavern at 1800 E Brown, **William's Inn,** it was also **Corner Tavern, Stallone's, Pink Poodle and Big Daddy's.** It's now the Capitol City Elks. Also in the East Side neighborhood was **Capital 19 Inn** at 1825 E Capital, it was also named **Steve's Place and Toni's** at one time. The **Mighty Fine Club, Maurer's and Jim & Toni's** were located at 2001 E Capital and **Fred's Club at** 2008 E Capital Avenue.

Wally's Tavern was located at 716 N 14th Street now the home of the Illinois Department of Corrections Administrative Offices.

Saners Tavern 1231 E Cook Leo Saner owner (1950)

The Fairview Club 2437 N 5th

We mentioned social clubs; to this day I'm not sure how they operated legally maybe they didn't but I did have occasion to visit a club owned by Cozi Coe near 11th and Cook Street but don't recall the name. I met a guy there called "Falstaff Rich", you can guess why.

Another social club was located at 1629 E Carpenter, **Peggy's Over 30 Club.** I also remember the **JAX 11,** I think it was located near 11th and Jackson St, but couldn't find a liquor license for it; maybe that wasn't that unusual back in the day.

Taverns near the corner of 11th and Cook were **The Keyhole and Jonnie and Jan's** at 605 S 11[th,] **Kaspers** at 625 S 11[th.] · The well-known original **Office Tavern** was located at 631 S 11th Street.

On East Jackson Street locals frequented **Barney and Ann's** later **Sully's; Bob's Tavern** at 1112 E Jackson and the **Jackson Street Inn at** 1128 E Jackson. At 2001 E Jackson was **Steve and Don's, Sully's, Chuck and Dots, Postal Lounge and the Bullfrog Inn.** Sandra Grounds wrote to us and said Sully was her dad and he held the second oldest county liquor license and one of the first 3:00 am licenses in town, She said. "Dad was the first to bring scopitone to Sangamon County. The machine was like a jukebox with a video. He had that at his 2801 Peoria Rd. location. He had live entertainment at that location for a while and the fiddle player ended up touring with Dolly Parton. His name was Tommy Rutledge."

If you traveled East on Clear Lake you would have found 1930 E Clear Lake home to **Termine's, Bill and Elma's The Country Corner and later Paddy's Place.** The building has been demolished but the memories remain forever. Almost attached to Termine's was **Bianco's** Little Supper Club at 1926 Clear Lake; it's still standing but shouldn't be; Dominic Bianco owned it.

Just down the street was **The Hi-Lo, Bobby Darren's, AKIS and the County Line Bar** at 2710 Clear Lake, **Ray's Tavern** at 2718 Clear Lake and near the corner of East Clear Lake and 31st Street you found **The Southern Aire,** the **Parkview Club** (now Mario's) at 3073 Clear Lake and at 3129 **Ferrel's Corner,** later the Ponderosa Steak House. Before chain restaurants like the Ponderosa existed folks raved about **Babe and Jims** located at 3027 Clear Lake. Nearby was **The Embers** at 3129 Clearlake.

It was across the street from Shaheen's raceway at the U.S. 66 by pass and Clearlake Ave. Young drivers like NASCAR legend Jeff Gordon raced at Shaheen's on any given Saturday night. Joe Shaheen was a Springfield legend and operated the raceway from 1947-1988.

Do you remember **Ben's Place, Converse Club, Converse Tavern, Don's Corner, Bill and Fanny's or HOD's Place** located at 1601 East Converse?

A little further on East Enos was **Andrew's Tavern** at 716 E Enos, it was later owned and operated by Suzie Weiss, better know as **Suzie Q's.** Suzie was and still is an icon in the bar business.

My Brother's Place at 1028 E Enos, but many will remember taverns once located at 1030 E Enos; **Boehning's, Down's, Ruble's Tavern and Wally's.**

At 1031 South Grand Ave East an iconic tavern still stands; **Bookers Tavern** located there since 1934. On any given night at Bookers you might find local politicians meeting to discuss election strategy or the owners and employees of Evans and Mason Masonry Contractors determining their bid for the next large construction project.

Rich Bruce, (one of 12 kids) bought Bookers (**Bernie's**) and called it **Bruce's** and it's now the **Bourbon Street Rhythm and Blues.**

Going east at 1117 E So Grand you would have found **Butchers** later **The Cracked Crock.** Is it just me or were there some real characters in the cracked crock.

The **Rialto, Sandridge and the South Town Lounge** were located at 1124 So Grand E and at 2200 So Grand E was **Pokora's** and **Wilsons** now the **G&M Package Liquor and Lounge.**

The Green Wienie 2805 E Cook

Chuck and Dot's 2001 E Jackson (1967)

The West, Central and Some South Neighborhood's

A wonderful woman and great friend helped us recall some of the west side memories for this book; Mrs. Betty Ruth Hart lived in the neighborhood near **Ollie's Tavern, (Ollie and Mae's)** located at 2815 Price Street. Betty and her husband owned SMW automotive specialty paints; their shop was at 100 W Jefferson, which was the location of **Fassero's Tavern** before the paint shop.

Her son my good friend Mike Hart owned and operated First Street auto body there for over 30 years and as we write there is a rumor that the current owners of the **Butternut Hut** may be moving into the old First Street Auto body shop.

Also located on Price Street were **Lott's Tavern, Beelers Tap,** and **Price Street Pub**. In later years Marcel Brocardo who was part of the family that owned Vess soda company on S 15th and Melrose Street bought the place and called it **Marcel's Penny Bar.**

Another special mention goes to Pat Tavine who owned **Tavines** located on the SE corner of Wabash and Old Chatham Road. It was a big hangout for the Springfield Kings Hockey team and was formally **Michaels Supper Club,** it's now a Muffler shop. Pat went on to own and or manage several clubs like **The Lake Club** at 2820 Fox Bridge Rd., **Bombay Bicycle Club** (it was also **Gilligans**) on Dirksen Pky. and a few other downtown bars.

Speaking of the **Lake Club**, while it was a premier nightclub in the 50's and 60's local entertainers like **George Rank** were featured there for years. George later in life opened **George Ranks** at 6th and Laurel St.

Our friend Tommy Blasko ran the Lake Club before Pat Tavine. To this day Tommy will tell you the stories of "Rudy" the ghost who haunted the Lake Club. The story was featured on a national television show.

Just down the street from **Walt and Dene's** on Fox Road was the **Colony Club** at 2900 Fox Bridge Road and at 3000 Fox Road was **The Villa Valencia** in 1934.

Alfred "Curley" Hurrelbrink owned **Curley's",** a popular spot at 1033 Wabash, on the old Wabash Curve, it was the **Reno Club** before Curley bought it. Merle Hornstein owned the building, he was found brutally murdered in 1966 on the south side of Springfield.

Just around the curve were **Grier's Village Inn** at 1305 Wabash, and **The Becon/Coach Lite Inn** at 1311 Wabash. **The Wagon Wheel** was at 1531 Wabash, these were all near **The Moonlight Gardens Club and Roller rink** at 1800 Wabash.

Located near by at 1557 Wabash was **Nonnie's/ Suppan's,** it was next door to **The Cliff's** at 1577 Wabash. Near Old Chatham road at 1740 Wabash was **Bucks'/Little Joe's Club** and **Little Nino's.**

In the neighborhood was **Mr. Ed's** at 2700 So. Pasfield, (I thought it was on Highland?) remember that big horse standing on the billboard outside. It was also the **Jewel Lounge, Gillespie's** and **Harry's.**

I guess **Ada's Tavern** located at 807 W Maple Ave South would be considered west side.

Spencer's Tavern N Grand and Walnut

Henry's Tavern Jefferson and MacArthur

The Lake Club 2840 Fox Road. Tom Blasko and Bill Carmean

Lake Club New Years Eve 1947

Moon Light Gardens 1800 Wabash

O'Malley's Jefferson St

At 9th and South Grand Ave **The Georgian** was built in 1941 and torn down in 1986, a popular late night eatery for local tavern patrons. Does anyone recall the cook at the Georgian being arrested for the murder of a teenage girl whose body was dumped near the State Fairgrounds; he was never convicted of this horrible crime.

Mr. Ted's took the 3:15am breakfast trade over in later years.

Someone wrote to us on Facebook and asked the name of the tavern on the corner of 11th and Laurel, at one time it was the **Laurel Street Tavern,** but was best known as **Bill & Helens;** owned by Bill and Helen Reynolds. Drive by today and all you will find is the two concrete steps leading into the entrance. How many memories walked in and out on those steps!

Emil Rondelli owned taverns located at 2203 So. 15th Street way back in the day was **Emil and Angles, then Emil's, and Felber's.** Just across the street was **The White House** at 2170 So. 15th, later the **R Bar** and **The Club House. (Felbers Tavern** was also located at 1932 So. Grand East.)

A very special mention for the **49er** located at 1100 So 11th St, owned by John and Linda Bohan. In the late 70's thru the 80's Thursday was Cowboy Night, you got a free 49er plastic mug and paid to fill it with beer served by a local bartending favorite Nancy Hoyer. The place was packed! I have a lot of stories from the 49er, but then so does every neighborhood tavern patron. It was **Denk's Den** before the 49er. Butch Adish owned a classic **Lu's Home Tavern** 1031 So. 11th, just across the street from the 49er. John and Linda moved the 49er to the west side located at 518 Bruns Lane in the late 80's.

Another fine family Al and Nita Barnowsky owned and operated **Al's Corner** at 2028 So 11th. It was just down the block from **Rudy's Inn** at 1107 E Ash. Watt Brothers Pharmacy was just across the street. Further west, at 1008 E Ash was **Ellis U R Out Inn.** Larry Ellis was at one time a professional baseball umpire. Cutting across the center of the old city **Gabatoni's** at 300 Laurel still there and selling great pizza. **The Merry Go Round** was located at 2816 Lowell, and several hot spots were located at 2900 Lowell; they were; **Rosalie's Place, Dee's place, Maple Inn, DJ's Bar & Grill, Marge and Ben's** and **Suttons Landing.** Next door at 2901 Lowell was **Jackie's, Fred and Evelyn's** and **Brandenburgs.** Located on South MacArthur were; **The Par-A-Dice** at 1710, **Boulevard Liquor Store** at 1712 and the **Grand Inn** located at 2001 S MacArthur. Traveling south you would have found **Hogan's, Augie and Dino's and Bens Cocktail Lounge at** 2011 S MacArthur then **Quality Liquors** at 2013 S MacArthur. **The Green Lantern, Don and Henry's,** and **The Pub** were between 2100 and 2901 S MacArthur, and **The Inferno Lounge** was at 2907 S MacArthur.

Rettich's Supper Club 2302 N 15th (1950)

Sportsman's Lounge Mason and Rutledge

Bookers Tavern 11th and So. Grand Ed Ludwig owner

Bookers Tavern, Bartender (UK) worked there for 24 years

Bookers Tavern Christmas 1948

Conner's Tavern (1950)

We need to mention some great places located near the Center City and South Side as well!

John F. Herron operated **Herron's,** a tavern at 709 Spring, later **Herron's Golden Tap**. If you're from Springfield your may recall The **Midway Pub** on the NW corner of Spring and Cook Street, there are still peanut shells laying on the ground where it stood. It was across the street from **The Ideal Lounge.**

Eddie "Bunny" Carnduff was the owner of **The Oasis Tavern** at Spring and Cook St.

Just on the other side of the Capitol Complex was a local political hot spot in the 80's; **Play it Again Sam's** was located at 222 So. College the business was owned by a former State representative Sam Panionivich, Marilyn Kulavic tended bar there. In later years 70's -90's the politicians at least the Republicans moved to **D. H. Browns** at 3rd and Monroe St. Dave Brown Sr. a former WWII prisoner of war opened the place in 1977, it was later owned and operated by his son Dave Jr. and his daughter LuAnn and her husband Henry Kurth. On any given evening you would find lawyers, judges, cop's and even Governor James Thompson enjoying a cocktail together. You will still find Dave Jr. there most nights. The Democrats hung out at **Boone's Saloon** at that time, unlike today, they met in the middle-The Capitol Building, and got things done.

Another special mention should go to **Norb Andy's** at 518 E Capitol. Norb and Annalou Anderson ran the place successfully for over 40 years. Tim Nudo owned **The Bedrock Bar** at 225 Monroe St. You could find Bob Schleyhann and Buck Westen belly up to the bar most Saturdays.

One of Springfield's favorites **Two Brothers Lounge** owned by Wally Hirstein was and still stands at 413 E Monroe. Wally operated the place for over 35 years (1947-1982) and sold it to Tommy Heck who along with his wife Brenda operated the hot spot successfully for about 5 years. After that a few others operated the bar at that location but unfortunately it's closed.

The Springfield area tavern business really changed in the 80'-90's thanks to four local bar owners; Wally Hirstein owner of **Two Brothers**, John Bohan owner of the **49ER**, Dave Brown Jr. owner of **DH Browns** and Dr. Paul Mahon an Irish immigrant and owner of **Same O'le Shillelagh.** 951 S Durkin Dr.

These four friends socialized together and also stopped by each other's business on a regular basis. This was unlike the old neighborhood taverns where most everyone stayed in their neighborhood. The four of them started a local tradition in the 80's called the **Four Bar Open** golf outing. This gave birth to golf outings hosted by local bar's, a tradition still going on today.

Traveling south on the main drag, 6th Street you would have found **Poland's Tavern** located at 2620 South Sixth. **Fidlers Tavern** was located at 2715 So. 6th and **Fritz's Place** was located at 211 So. 6th. **The Roxy Tavern** (There were two Roxy taverns at the same time) was at 419 South Fifth Street and **The Sazarac** was located at 229 So. 6th. The **Ritz Inn** was located at 2240 S 6th, next door to a Springfield favorite **The Black Angus,** now closed and for sale at 2241 So 6th. Just across the parking lot was **The Elbow Room,** also called **Dicks Lounge and JW's Lounge** at 2266 So 6th Street.

Further south you would have found a very unique place **Davis and Turley's** at 2640 So 6th. The owners collected old classic cars and stored them above the hardware store/tavern. It wasn't until I was older when I realized my dad went to the hardware store a lot but he never fixed anything at home! Across the street was another Springfield icon, **The Supper Club** at 2641 So 6th, it was later operated by **Louie Smarjesse,** a class gentleman.

In the opening remarks I mentioned Homeier's dairy; In the 1980's I believe Shepardo's Pizza opened at the old dairy location, after that a gentleman named Archie Maxwell opened **Archies Cove** and at least for a short time and in the 80's or 90's the old dairy was **Callies Bar.** A good friend and Springfield classic Jim Canfield stopped by Callies on occasion. Jim passed away October 31st, 2018.

Two Brothers Lounge 413 E Monroe Wally Hirstein Owner

D.H. Browns 3rd and Monroe

The Plantation, The Orchid Lounge and **The End Zone,** were located at 2701, 2715 and 2765 So. 6th, about where County Market is today. Located at 2805 So 6th was **Gathard's Pkg. Liquor** later **Kings Package Liquor and Tavern,** and the iconic **Curve Inn** still open and packed with good people at 3219 So Sixth Street Road.

Further south at 1220 Toronto Road, originally The Crows Mill School built in the 1900's was later the original **Navy Club** and was operated by the Gathard family. Paul Marconi later opened it as **Bootleggers,** and now its re-opened as the **Crows Mill Pub,** a popular place owned by our friend Scott and Theresa Weitekamp. There were various owners in between the original school and the current Pub.

If you ever spent a night at **The Aloha** a former Texaco gas station at South Sixth and St. Joseph St. just outside the city limits and if you can remember it, you met Myles Ries **"Myles"** the piano player and owner operator sisters **Elda** Blalock and **Novella** Pacotti. The drinks were strong especially the Flaming Hurricane, the music was loud so were those corn filled beer cans. Everyone left there with a great story. Some of the other regular characters were bartender "Mort the patch wearer", Mort Lucas and "Jimmy" the queer. If you went to the Aloha you were looking for a good time and you most likely found it, maybe more. In December of 1989 the Illinois Liquor Commission and the Illinois Department of Public Health shut the place down for "violations, unclean and unsanitary conditions". Again if you were ever there you know that's not a stretch! In just a few short years the owners, and patrons were able to establish a Springfield Icon!

We have a few PG rated pictures of the Aloha.

Orchid Lounge, 2715 South Sixth, Springfield, Ill.

The Orchid Lounge 2715 South Sixth

McCaffrey's Saloon 1326 S 11th (1902)

Archie's Cove Stanford Ave Archie Maxwell owner

The Oasis Tavern Spring and Cook Eddie "Bunny" Carnduff owner

*Norb Andy Tabarin
Norb and Anna Lou
Anderson owners*

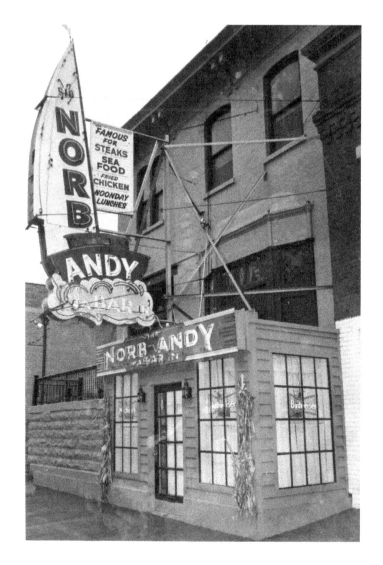

Chantilly Lace 5th and Stanford

The Aloha 6th St at St. Joseph St

The Aloha Music by Myles

The Aloha proprietors

The Aloha- "Can of Corn"

The Aloha "The Mix-ologist"

"The Flaming Blue Hawaiian"

Brewery's- Beer Distributors- Bartenders

The rich history Springfield Illinois enjoys surrounding its local taverns extend to the foundation of the beer industry, its Brewery's and its Beer distributors. An article published in the "American Breweriana Journal" in 2009 said that the first brewery in Springfield was the **Busher's Springfield Brewery,** (1840-1860). Their advertisements indicated John Busher Jr. was a "rectifier and wholesale dealer in Ale, Porter and Lager", their address listed as "opposite the Journal Office, Springfield Illinois.

The Kun, Rudolph & Keydell Brewery (1857-1877) came to Springfield from St. Louis. Andrew Kun operated his brewery at the west end of Reynolds Street until he passed in 1863. He leased facilities from the Reisch Brewery during the prohibition scare when Franz Reisch was not willing to break the law. Kun's wife Rosa later married Robert Rudolph a brewer employed at their brewery. The Rudolph's built a mansion at 511 Carpenter St later called the Diller Mansion until it was torn down in 1968. Kun's legacy lived on when in 1993 construction workers discovered a sinkhole on Walnut Street just north of Carpenter about twenty feet under the road. An archeological team later discovered the large 18 feet x 103 feet caverns were part of Kun's brewery storage cellars. Moritz Keydell leased the brewery from the Rudolph's in 1870.

The Herman & Laubheimer Brewery (1865-1873) was located near the southwest corner of Jefferson and Amos Street. A second owner Fredrick C Herman sold a portion of the brewery to John Laubheimer (Lobehamer) in 1868; he bought out Herman in 1869.

Henry Long's Brewery (1865-1871) was located near Fayette and Feldkamp Street. The Feldkamps for whom the street was named were neighbors to Henry Long.

Ackerman & Nolte- City Park Brewery (1864-1880). Phillip Ackerman was born in Germany in 1828 and moved to Springfield in 1853, he bought property at Mason and Reynolds Street, which soon became the location of his brewery. August Nolte was made a partner in 1869.

While there were a few other start up brewery's in Springfield such as Charles Weist at 2nd and Reynolds and August Brana and the **White Beer Brewing Company** located on Monroe between 4th and 5th, they failed to compare with two Springfield success stories.

The Springfield Brewing Company, 1030 E Madison a post prohibition startup began in 1933 and was a huge success producing it's **Archer Beer,** then **Engelking's** a lower priced beer. They produced several other brands but an A.B.A article indicated, "Most if not all were the same beer". Springfield Brewing closed in 1940.

Springfield Brewing Company 1030 E Mason

Springfield Brewery Englekings Beer Brew Masters

Englekings Beer Quality Control

Springfield Brewery Quality Control

Engelkings Beer Sales

The Reisch Brewing Company 723 N Rutledge was by far the most successful; Franz Sales Reisch started the business in 1849. The Reisch family embraced the German American tradition of beer production and George Reisch a sixth generation brewer, followed the family tradition as a brewer for Anheuser-Busch in St. Louis. The Reisch Brewery closed in 1966. Its remains were discovered over and over again during the construction of the SIU School of Medicine.

In January 2019 the Reisch family announced they are bringing back **Reisch Gold Top Beer** and should be for sale in the Springfield Illinois market in 2019.

With the closing of the Reisch Brewery, the king of brewery's, local brewing lost it's charm. But in 1994 Bruce "Buddy" Hunter opened **Capital City Brewing Company** at 107 W Cook St. It closed in 1998, but continued as a restaurant. Now craft beer's and local brewing are the rage.

Following are several old photographs of the brewery's and brewing operations.

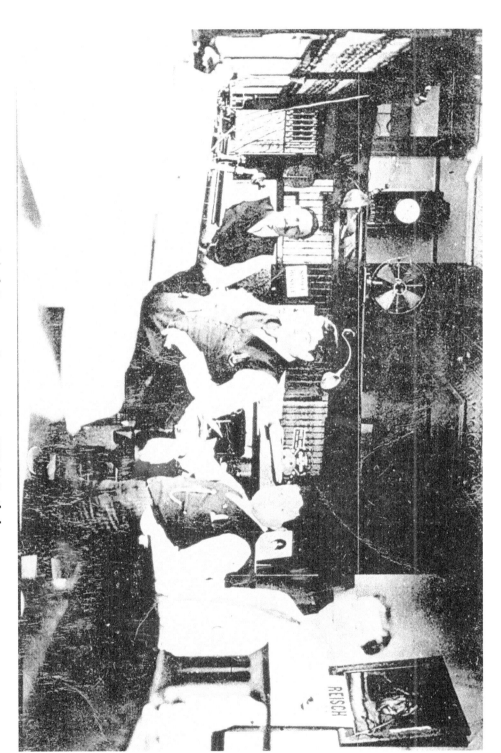

Reisch Brewery Brew masters 723 N Rutledge

Reisch Brewery Factory 723 N Rutledge

Reisch Brewery operations

Reisch Brewery Storage Vat's

Reisch Brewery Malt Extract

Reisch Brewery Keg operations

Reisch Brewery Delivery

Reisch Brewery Delivery in the early years

Reisch Brewery delivery- Notice the chain drive on the trucks

Beer Distributors

With all the local brewery's producing these high quality lager's and with Brewery giants in nearby St. Louis Missouri and Peoria Illinois, it didn't take long especially after prohibition for entrepreneurs to figure out there was money to be made distributing the product, first by horse and wagon, then truck and trailer. Some of the beer distributors that were around in the 1930's were;

- **Joe Schafer and Son's** 1st and Madison distributors of Anheuser-Busch products.
- **J P Dunn, Ice and Coal**-2nd and Madison distributors of Dicks Quincy Beer.
- **Edelweiss Distributing**-230 N Second St.
- **Heidelberg Distributing** 825 E Adams St.
- **Highland Distributing** 415 E Washington St. distributors on Highland Beer.
- **Kohlbecker & Bradley Distributors** 403 N Fourth, distributors of Blue Ribbon Beer.
- **Mester Bottling Co.** 320 N Sixth, distributors of Griesediech and Champagne Velvet
- **John Mussatto** 214 N Fourth distributor of Cooks Gold Blume
- **Prima Beer Distributing** 917 E Jackson
- **Schott Brewing** 221 N Sixth distributor of Highland Beer
- **Starr Brothers** 1016 E Ash distributors of Falstaff Beer
- **Steele & Hederich** 603 S 11th, distributors of Old Style Lager and Meister Brau
- **Tony Yucus** 1700 Sangamon Ave, distributors of Bismark and Old Manhattan

Bartenders A Family Tradition

There are far too many memorable bartenders to mention, most likely because every watering hole had its favorite, I'm sure an entire book could be dedicated to the wonderful bartenders who have served us over the last 100 years. Several of the family owned husband and wife teams have been mentioned, like **Jonny and Vi Riba** at 2800 S 11ᵗʰ, even husbands and wives in the same location such and **Mike Ushman and Dea Galassi –Ushman and Walt and "Haroldene" Dene Antonacci** at 2790 Fox Road.

Again I know each and every tavern has its favorite bartenders but these and a few other originals deserve special mention. They were pioneers in the tavern business in Springfield of one sort or another.

Ed and George Endres, Endres Tavern at 1047 Stanford, **John B Hagan** 1221 Linn ST. **Lake Springfield Tavern, Charlie Zaubi of Charlie's Tavern** 1041 Stanford. **Edwin Dahlkamp of the Cottage Inn.**

The Manci Family, Guido, Angelo, Henry & Louie Jr. with other family members have been in the tavern business in Springfield for over 75 years. Henry Manci wrote to us and said at one time the Manci family owned **Emils, Hi-D Ho, Lincoln Square Tavern, Brooklyn Tavern, The Travel Inn** and **The Curve Inn** all at the same time. I'd say this family was one of the pioneers of the tavern business in Springfield. You can still find "Poor Louie" Manci Jr. tending bar at his place **Louies Bar and Beer Garden** everyday.

Some of the other families and owner operators include **The Marconi Family, Louie Smarjesse, Manny and Martin Baptist, Carl Pokora,** all owned or operated famous places in or nearby Springfield. **Alfred "Curly" Hurrelbrink** was an icon in the bar business, as was **Buster DiNora. Emil Saccaro** and the **Sacarro Family** owned several establishments around town. Lets not forget the **Impastato, Rondelli, Delleo, Zito and Machino families.** There are so many more, please contact us with your memories.

From the 1930's to today, local bar owners and bartenders and beer and liquor distributors have made a difference in peoples lives, always willing to listen to or tell a story and to have one more with you. A few other people owning, working or distributing to the local bars that we want to remember in addition to those listed throughout the book, some more than once are;

Tom Egizii, E & F Distributing, Bob Schafer, Pete Orlindini, Ron "RCA" Adams, Bob Ginder, Bob Schleyhahn, Jack Kelly, Mac Frazier, Dave Brown Sr., Big Betty from the Supper Club and the Chickie Bar in Marco Island, Linda "Red" from DHB, Suzie "Q" Weiss, "Sweed", Pete Welch, Marcel Brocardo Wally Hirstein, Dave Brown Jr. and John Bohan. Also special mentions go to Jamie Tavine and Lloyd "Butch" Staber still working hard in the tavern business.

3 O'clock Liquor License Taverns

A story has been told "back in the day" if the police received a call reporting a fight or some trouble in a bar late night the Springfield City Police sent John Graves and or Gene Truax and the county sent Chico Belle; Problem Solved! Interestingly, Chico Belle was later a bouncer at the Lake Club and Gene Truax drove a Beer delivery transport for Schafer's, the Budweiser distributor. A few of the "just outside city limits" Three O Clock bars were;

The Blue Moon, owned by Eric and Clara Schmidt was at 2300 Peoria Rd, **The Mighty Fine** at 3045 Sangamon Ave. Marino Mazzini owned the **Wishing Well** at 3036 N Peoria Rd, and Nellie Pelc owned the **Crawdad Hole** near Peoria Rd and Sherman road. Ben Jewel owned **Ben's** 2011 S MacArthur, deserving a second mention is the **Skyrocket** owned by Peter Welsh 2200 Peoria Rd.

Tavern Talk Memories.

The goal of this small book is to get some "Tavern Talk" started. We are well aware some taverns are not listed and that we may have some listed incorrectly although we tried to verify the information we were able to gather. There are a lot of compiled "lists" and the city directory that simply provide the name and address of old city taverns but we would really like the stories behind the taverns name, owners and the address. Our sincere hope is that this book will generate some great conversations and memories.

Please contact us with any corrections and especially with your photos, stories and memories.

Tavern Talk II will include other iconic taverns in and around Springfield as well as more of the great places in Sangamon County.

We believe it's important to document these historic places and their place in our history. Many of our cities "founders" are aging and we need to hear their stories in detail before they are no longer available to us. So sit down and have a beer with some old codger, listen to their "back in the day" stories; they are truly important.

Thanks to everyone that participated !
Bobby & Sandy Orr
Like us on Facebook-"Springfield Tavern History"
E-Mail: Taverntalkspi@gmail.com or mcgregorr@aol.com

"The Manci, Viola, Alfonsi and Rondelli Families at Emil's Tavern 15th and Cornell St (1940's)

CPSIA information can be obtained
at www.ICGtesting.com
Printed in the USA
BVHW090827150919
558469BV00012B/53/P

9 781478 780380

THE PROUD NORTH END TAVERNS